Low Carb Coc Beginn

Delicious Beginner Friendly Low Carb Recipes For Burning Fat

Copyright ©

Disclaimer

All the material contained in this book is provided for educational and informational purposes only. No responsibility can be taken for any results or outcomes resulting from the use of this material.

While every attempt has been made to provide information that is both accurate and effective, the author does not assume any responsibility for the accuracy or use/misuse of this information.

Table of Contents

Roasted Herbed Turkey

Juicy Slow Cooked Roast Beef

Delicious Herbed Chicken Breasts

Roasted Herbed Lemon Chicken

Dill Salmon

Creamy Dijon Chicken

Stuffed Pork Chops

Grilled Lemon Pork Chops

Rosemary Pork Loin Roast

Goat Cheese Chicken Breasts

Introduction

The low carb diet has been proven to be one of the best diets for losing weight. Many studies show that consuming more carbs leads to more weight gain and obesity. The recipes in this cookbook are all low in carbohydrates, and will help you lose weight by limiting your daily intake of carbs. This low carb cookbook contains delicious recipes for all meals of the day, and also has many beginner friendly low carb recipes for you to enjoy.

Good luck and we hope you enjoy these delicious low carb recipes for helping you burn fat and lose weight!

Chapter 1: Low Carb Breakfast Recipes

Low Carb Cream Cheese Crepes

Ingredients

3 ounces cream cheese, softened

2 eggs, beaten

1 teaspoon ground cinnamon

1 tablespoon sugar-free syrup

1 teaspoon butter

Directions

In a bowl, mash the cream cheese with beaten eggs, about 1 teaspoon at a time at first, until the mixture is smooth and free of lumps. Beat in the cinnamon and sugar-free syrup.

Melt the butter in a nonstick skillet over medium heat. When the butter has stopped foaming, reduce heat to medium-low, and pour in several tablespoons of the batter.

Swirl to coat the bottom of the skillet. Allow to cook until set, about 4 minutes on the first side; flip the crepe with a spatula and cook the other side until the crepe shows small browned spots, 1 to 2 more minutes.

Nutrition:

Calories 241; Fat 21g; Protein 10g; Carbs 2; per 1/2 recipe

Cheesy Baked Green Onion Omelet

Ingredients

1 teaspoon butter

9 large eggs

1/2 cup sour cream

1/2 cup milk

1 teaspoon salt

2 green onions, chopped

1/4 cup shredded Cheddar cheese

Directions

Preheat oven to 350 degrees F (175 degrees C). Grease an 8x8-inch baking dish with butter.

Beat eggs, sour cream, milk, and salt in a bowl until blended. Stir in green onions. Pour mixture in the prepared baking dish.

Bake in the preheated oven until set, 25 to 30 minutes. Sprinkle Cheddar cheese over eggs and continue baking until cheese is melted, 2 to 3 minutes more.

Nutrition:

Calories 185; Fat 14g; Protein 12g; Carbs 3; per 1/6 recipe

Cream Cheese Tomato Omelet

Ingredients

2 eggs

1 tablespoon milk

salt and ground black pepper to taste

3 tablespoons cream cheese, softened

2 tablespoons seeded and diced tomato

1 tablespoon chopped fresh chives

Directions

Whisk eggs, milk, salt, and pepper together in a bowl.

Heat a 6-inch nonstick skillet over medium heat; pour egg mixture into the hot skillet, tilting so egg mixture covers the entire bottom of skillet. Slowly cook egg mixture until set, 5 to 10 minutes.

Arrange small dollops of cream cheese onto half the omelet; sprinkle tomato and chives over cream cheese.

Fold omelet in half over the fillings. Remove skillet from heat and cover until cream cheese has softened, 2 to 3 minutes.

Nutrition:

Calories 260; Fat 21g; Protein 16g; Carbs 3; per recipe

Savory Zucchini Pancakes

Ingredients

1 pound zucchini, grated

salt to taste

1/4 cup freshly grated Parmesan cheese

2 eggs

2 green onions, chopped

3 cloves garlic, chopped

4 leaves basil, chopped

1 pinch ground nutmeg

1 pinch onion powder

ground black pepper to taste

1 tablespoon butter

1 teaspoon olive oil, or as needed

Directions

Squeeze grated zucchini in paper towels to release as much water as possible. Spread zucchini on fresh paper towels and sprinkle with salt; let sit for 30 minutes to release additional water; squeeze again.

Mix Parmesan cheese, eggs, green onions, garlic, basil, nutmeg, onion powder, and black pepper in a bowl; add zucchini. Stir to combine.

Heat butter and olive oil in a frying pan over medium heat. Form golf ball-sized zucchini patties and place in hot frying pan.

Fry until browned, 2 to 3 minutes per side.

Nutrition:

Calories 115; Fat 8g; Protein 6g; Carbs 6; per 1/4 recipe

Easy Cream Cheese Pancakes

Ingredients

2 eggs

2 ounces cream cheese, softened

1 packet stevia

1/2 teaspoon ground cinnamon

Directions

Combine eggs, cream cheese, stevia, and cinnamon in a blender; blend until smooth. Let batter sit until bubbles settle, about 2 minutes.

Heat a large skillet over medium heat. Pour 1/4 of the batter onto the skillet; cook until golden brown, about 2 minutes.

Flip and continue cooking until second side is golden brown, about 1 minute more. Repeat with remaining batter.

Nutrition:

Calories 86; Fat 7g; Protein 4g; Carbs 1; per 1/4 recipe

Sweet Onion And Bacon Omelet

Ingredients

4 strips bacon

1 teaspoon butter

1/2 sweet onion, diced

3 jumbo eggs

2 tablespoons water

1/4 cup shredded sharp Cheddar cheese

1 slice process American cheese, diced

1/8 teaspoon salt

1/8 teaspoon crushed red pepper flakes

Directions

Cook bacon in a skillet over medium-high heat until crisp. Remove with a slotted spoon to paper towels to drain and cool; crumble the bacon and set aside.

Melt the butter in a skillet over medium heat. Cook and stir the onions in the butter until tender, about 10 minutes.

Prepare a 10-inch non-stick skillet with cooking spray and place over a cold burner. Whisk together the eggs and water; pour the egg mixture into the cold skillet.

Cover and turn the burner on for medium-low heat. Cook until steam begins to vent from the skillet. Remove the lid. Sprinkle the crumbled bacon, Cheddar cheese, American cheese, salt, and red pepper over the eggs.

Spread the onions over the eggs. Gently swirl the skillet in a circular motion to release the omelet and slide it onto a plate.

Fold the omelet in half. Allow the cheese to melt, about 2 minutes.

Nutrition:

Calories 380; Fat 29g; Protein 26g; Carbs 4; per 1/2 recipe

Almond Flour Pancakes

Ingredients

1/4 cup water

2 tablespoons almond flour

1 tablespoon vegetable oil

1 tablespoon heavy whipping cream

1 pinch baking powder

2 drops vanilla extract

1 egg

Directions

Whisk water, almond flour, vegetable oil, cream, baking powder, and vanilla extract together in a microwave-safe bowl.

Cook in the microwave on high until gooey batter forms, 1 1/2 to 2 minutes.

Let batter rest until cooled slightly, 1 to 2 minutes. Whisk in egg until well-blended.

Heat a lightly oiled griddle over medium-high heat. Drop batter onto the griddle and cook until bubbles form and the edges are dry, 4 to 5 minutes. Flip and cook until browned on the other side, 2 to 3 minutes. Repeat with remaining batter.

Nutrition:

Calories 340; Fat 32g; Protein 10g; Carbs 4; per recipe

Spinach Omelet

Ingredients

2 eggs

1 cup torn baby spinach leaves

1 1/2 tablespoons grated Parmesan cheese

1/8 teaspoon ground nutmeg

1/4 teaspoon onion powder

salt and pepper to taste

Directions

In a bowl, beat the eggs, and stir in the baby spinach and Parmesan cheese. Season with onion powder, nutmeg, salt, and pepper.

In a small skillet coated with cooking spray over medium heat, cook the egg mixture about 3 minutes, until partially set.

Flip with a spatula, and continue cooking 2 to 3 minutes. Reduce heat to low, and continue cooking 2 to 3 minutes, or to desired doneness.

Nutrition:

Calories 186; Fat 12g; Protein 16g; Carbs 3; per recipe

Cheesy Ham Breakfast Casserole

Ingredients

8 eggs

1 cup milk

salt and pepper to taste

2 cups diced ham

1 cup shredded cheddar cheese

Directions

Preheat oven to 350 degrees F (175 degrees C).

Beat eggs in a large bowl, making sure that they are mixed very well and have a 'frothy' top. Add the milk, salt and pepper. Mix well. Stir in ham, then add cheese pieces and stir well.

Pour mixture into a well greased 4 quart casserole dish and bake in the preheated oven for 50 to 60 minutes or until top is lightly browned.

Nutrition:

Calories 386; Fat 14g; Protein 15g; Carbs 4; per 1/4 of recipe

Greek Omelet

Ingredients

1 cup halved grape tomatoes

1 teaspoon dried oregano, divided

1/2 teaspoon salt, divided

Black pepper, to taste

1/2 cup crumbled feta cheese

8 large eggs

1 (10 ounce) package chopped frozen spinach, thawed and squeezed dry

1 tablespoon olive oil

Directions

Heat a 12-inch non-stick skillet over low heat. (Use a 10-inch skillet if you halve the recipe to serve 2 instead of 4.) Meanwhile, in a small bowl, mix tomatoes, 1/2 tsp. oregano, 1/4 tsp. salt, and pepper to taste. Stir in feta.

In a medium bowl, whisk eggs together, then stir in spinach, 1/2 tsp. oregano, 1/4 tsp. salt, and pepper to taste. A few minutes before cooking omelet, add oil to the pan, and increase heat to medium-high. Heat until wisps of smoke start to rise from the pan. Add the egg mixture to the skillet.

Using a plastic or wooden spatula to push back the eggs that have set, tilt the pan and let the uncooked egg mixture run onto the empty portion of the pan.

Continue pushing back cooked eggs, tilting the pan and letting uncooked egg mixture flow onto the empty portion of the pan until omelet is moist but fully cooked, about 3 minutes.

Reduce heat to low; pour the tomato mixture over half of the omelet. Using a slotted, flat spatula or turner, carefully fold the untopped half over the filling.

Use the turner to slide the omelet onto a cutting board. Let stand a minute or two for the filling to warm.

Cut the omelet into 4 wedges and serve immediately.

Nutrition:

Calories 253; Fat 18g; Protein 18g; Carbs 6; per 1/4 of recipe

Chapter 2: Low Carb Lunch Recipes

Crustless Ham Quiche

Ingredients

1 cup (not packed), non fat cottage cheese

2 cups egg whites

1/2 cup broccoli, cooked, chopped

1/2 cup ham, extra lean, (5% fat), diced

1/2 cup Cheddar or Colby Cheese, Low Fat, shredded

Salt and Pepper, to taste

Cooking Spray

Directions

Mix all ingredients in a large mixing bowl. Pour into a pie dish sprayed with Pam or other cooking spray.

Place on cookie sheet in oven. Bake approximately 45 minutes or until center is just set.

Nutrition:

Calories 106; Fat 1g; Protein 19g; Carbs 4g; per 1/6 of recipe

Spinach Quiche

Ingredients

1 tablespoon vegetable oil

1 onion, chopped

1 (10 ounce) package frozen chopped spinach, thawed and drained

5 eggs, beaten

3 cups shredded cheddar cheese

1/4 teaspoon salt

1/8 teaspoon ground black pepper

Directions

Preheat oven to 350 degrees F (175 degrees C). Lightly grease a 9 inch pie pan.

Heat oil in a large skillet over medium-high heat. Add onions and cook, stirring occasionally, until onions are soft. Stir in spinach and continue cooking until excess moisture has evaporated.

In a large bowl, combine eggs, cheese, salt and pepper. Add spinach mixture and stir to blend. Scoop into prepared pie pan.

Bake in preheated oven until eggs have set, about 30 minutes. Let cool for 10 minutes before serving.

Nutrition:

Calories 309; Fat 24g; Protein 20g; Carbs 5g; per 1/6 of recipe

Creamy Cauliflower Casserole

Ingredients

16 oz bag frozen cauliflower

2 tbsp butter

4 oz cream cheese, softened

1 lb turkey bacon, cooked until crispy and crumbled

8 oz shredded sharp cheddar cheese, divided

2 tbsp chopped green onions

2 tbsp Water

Directions

Microwave cauliflower with 2 tbsp water for 10-15 minutes until very soft, drain, then mash with potato masher.

Blend in butter and cream cheese.

Add the shredded cheese (reserving about 1/2 cup) and remaining ingredients, and stir together.

Put in a casserole dish and top with remaining shredded cheese.

Bake 350 for 20 minutes, until brown and bubbly.

Nutrition:

Calories 165; Fat 12g; Protein 10g; Carbs 3g; per 1/8 of recipe

Cheesy Broccoli Casserole

Ingredients

1 (10.75 ounce) can condensed cream of mushroom soup

1 cup mayonnaise

1 egg, beaten

1/4 cup finely chopped onion

3 (10 ounce) packages frozen chopped broccoli

8 ounces shredded sharp Cheddar cheese

salt to taste

ground black pepper to taste

2 pinches paprika

Directions

Preheat oven to 350 degrees F (175 degrees C). Butter a 9x13 inch baking dish.

In a medium bowl, whisk together condensed cream of mushroom soup, mayonnaise, egg and onion.

Place frozen broccoli into a very large mixing bowl. (I like to use my large stainless steel bowl to mix this recipe thoroughly.) Break up the frozen broccoli. Using a rubber spatula, scrape soup-mayonnaise mixture on top of broccoli, and mix well. Sprinkle on cheese and mix well. Spread mixture into prepared baking dish, and smooth top of casserole. Season to taste with salt, pepper and paprika.

Bake for 45 minutes to 1 hour in the preheated oven.

Nutrition:

Calories 387; Fat 34g; Protein 9.5g; Carbs 11g; per 1/8 of recipe

Creamy Mushroom Soup

Ingredients

8 ounces fresh mushrooms

2 tablespoons onions, chopped

1 -2 garlic clove, minced

2 tablespoons butter

2 tablespoons flour (separated)

2 cups chicken broth

1 cup light cream or 1 cup evaporated milk

½ teaspoon salt

¼ teaspoon pepper

¼ teaspoon nutmeg

Directions

Cut the mushrooms into slices.

Melt butter in large frying pan. Add in onions, garlic, and mushrooms. Cook until onions are soft.

Blend in 1 tbsp flour and stir.

Add in the chicken broth and heat until slightly thickened while stirring frequently.

Stir cream with additional 1 tbsp flour and seasonings. Add in cream to soup. Heat to thicken while stirring frequently.

Nutrition:

Calories 146; Fat 12g; Protein 4g; Carbs 6g; per 1/6 of recipe

Cheesy Stuffed Jalapenos

Ingredients

1 pound ground pork sausage

1 (8 ounce) package cream cheese, softened

1 cup shredded Parmesan cheese

1 pound large fresh jalapeno peppers, halved lengthwise and seeded

Directions

Preheat oven to 425 degrees F (220 degrees C).

Place sausage in a skillet over medium heat, and cook until evenly brown. Drain grease.

In a bowl, mix the sausage, cream cheese, and Parmesan cheese. Spoon about 1 tablespoon sausage mixture into each jalapeno half. Arrange stuffed halves in baking dishes.

Bake 20 minutes in the preheated oven, until bubbly and lightly browned.

Nutrition:

Calories 362; Fat 34g; Protein 9g; Carbs 4g; per 1/12 of recipe

Bacon And Green Beans

Ingredients

6 thick slices bacon, chopped

1/2 cup onions, minced

1 teaspoon minced garlic

1 pound fresh green beans, trimmed

1 cup water

1/8 teaspoon salt

1 pinch ground black pepper

Directions

Place bacon in a large, deep skillet. Cook over medium high heat until the fat begins to render.

Stir in onions and garlic; let cook for 1 minute. Stir in beans and water. Let the beans cook until the water has evaporated and the beans are tender.

If the beans are not tender once the water has evaporated, add a small amount more water and let them cook until tender.

Season with salt and pepper and serve.

Nutrition:

Calories 97; Fat 5g; Protein 6g; Carbs 7g; per 1/6 of recipe

Chapter 3: Low Carb Dinner Recipes

Grilled Spicy Chicken Breasts

Ingredients

2 1/2 tablespoons paprika

2 tablespoons garlic powder

1 tablespoon salt

1 tablespoon onion powder

1 tablespoon dried thyme

1 tablespoon ground cayenne pepper

1 tablespoon ground black pepper

4 skinless, boneless chicken breast halves

Directions

In a medium bowl, mix together the paprika, garlic powder, salt, onion powder, thyme, cayenne pepper, and ground black pepper.

Preheat grill for medium-high heat. Rub some of the reserved 3 tablespoons of seasoning onto both sides of the chicken breasts.

Lightly oil the grill grate. Place chicken on the grill, and cook for 6 to 8 minutes on each side, until juices run clear.

Nutrition:

Calories 173; Fat 2g; Protein 29g; Carbs 9g; per 1/4 of recipe

Roasted Herbed Turkey

Ingredients

1 (12 pound) whole turkey

3/4 cup olive oil

2 tablespoons garlic powder

2 teaspoons dried basil

1 teaspoon ground sage

1 teaspoon salt

1/2 teaspoon black pepper

2 cups water

Directions

Preheat oven to 325 degrees F (165 degrees C). Clean turkey, discard giblets and organs, and place in a roasting pan with a lid.

In a small bowl, combine olive oil, garlic powder, dried basil, ground sage, salt, and black pepper. Using a basting brush, apply the mixture to the outside of the uncooked turkey. Pour water into the bottom of the roasting pan, and cover.

Bake for 3 to 3 1/2 hours, or until the internal temperature of the thickest part of the thigh measures 180 degrees F (82 degrees C). Remove bird from oven, and allow to stand for about 30 minutes before carving.

Nutrition:

Calories 597; Fat 33g; Protein 68g; Carbs 1g; per 1/16 of recipe

Juicy Slow Cooked Roast Beef

Ingredients

1/3 cup soy sauce

1 (1 ounce) package dry onion soup mix

3 pounds beef chuck roast

2 teaspoons freshly ground black pepper

Directions

Pour soy sauce and dry onion soup mix into the slow cooker; mix well. Place chuck roast into the slow cooker. Add water until the top 1/2 inch of the roast is not covered. Sprinkle ground pepper on top.

Cover and cook on low for 22 hours.

Nutrition:

Calories 555; Fat 40g; Protein 40g; Carbs 4g; per 1/6 of recipe

Delicious Herbed Chicken Breasts

Ingredients

3 tablespoons olive oil

1 tablespoon minced onion

1 clove crushed garlic

1 teaspoon dried thyme

1/2 teaspoon dried rosemary, crushed

1/4 teaspoon ground sage

1/4 teaspoon dried marjoram

1/2 teaspoon salt

1/2 teaspoon ground black pepper

1/8 teaspoon hot pepper sauce

4 bone-in chicken breast halves, with skin

1 1/2 tablespoons chopped fresh parsley

Directions

Preheat oven to 425 degrees F (220 degrees C).

In a bowl, prepare the basting sauce by combining olive oil, onion, garlic, thyme, rosemary, sage, marjoram, salt, pepper, and hot pepper sauce.

Turn chicken breasts in sauce to coat thoroughly. Place skin side up in a shallow baking dish. Cover.

Roast at 425 degrees F (220 degrees C), basting occasionally with pan drippings, for about 35 to 45 minutes.

Remove to warm platter, spoon pan juices over, and sprinkle with fresh parsley.

Nutrition:

Calories 391; Fat 22g; Protein 45g; Carbs 1g; per 1/4 of recipe

Roasted Herbed Lemon Chicken

Ingredients

2 teaspoons Italian seasoning

1/2 teaspoon seasoning salt

1/2 teaspoon mustard powder

1 teaspoon garlic powder

1/2 teaspoon ground black pepper

1 (3 pound) whole chicken

2 lemons

2 tablespoons olive oil

Directions

Preheat oven to 350 degrees F (175 degrees C).

Combine the seasoning, salt, mustard powder, garlic powder and black pepper; set aside. Rinse the chicken thoroughly, and remove the giblets. Place chicken in a 9x13 inch baking dish. Sprinkle 1 1/2 teaspoons of the spice mixture inside the chicken. Rub the remaining mixture on the outside of the chicken.

Squeeze the juice of the 2 lemons into a small bowl or cup, and mix with the olive oil. Drizzle this oil/juice mixture over the chicken.

Bake in the preheated oven for 1 1/2 hours, or until juices run clear, basting several times with the remaining oil mixture.

Nutrition:

Calories 405; Fat 29g; Protein 32g; Carbs 4g; per 1/8 of recipe

Dill Salmon

Ingredients

1 pound salmon fillets

1/4 teaspoon salt

1/2 teaspoon ground black pepper

1 teaspoon onion powder

1 teaspoon dried dill weed

2 tablespoons butter

Directions

Preheat oven to 400 degrees F (200 degrees C).

Rinse salmon, and arrange in a 9x13 inch baking dish. Sprinkle salt, pepper, onion powder, and dill over the fish. Place pieces of butter evenly over the fish.

Bake in preheated oven for 20 to 25 minutes. Salmon is done when it flakes easily with a fork

Nutrition:

Calories 262; Fat 18g; Protein 23g; Carbs 1g; per 1/4 of recipe

Creamy Dijon Chicken

Ingredients

1 tablespoon butter

1 tablespoon olive oil

4 skinless, boneless chicken breast halves

salt and pepper to taste

1/2 cup heavy cream

1 tablespoon Dijon mustard

2 teaspoons chopped fresh tarragon

Directions

Melt the butter and heat the oil in a skillet over medium-high heat. Season chicken with salt and pepper, and place in the skillet.

Brown on both sides. Reduce heat to medium, cover, and continue cooking 15 minutes, or until chicken juices run clear. Set aside and keep warm.

Stir cream into the pan, scraping up brown bits. Mix in mustard and tarragon. Cook and stir 5 minutes, or until thickened.

Return chicken to skillet to coat with sauce. Drizzle chicken with remaining sauce to serve.

Nutrition:

Calories 310; Fat 21g; Protein 27g; Carbs 2g; per 1/4 of recipe

Stuffed Pork Chops

Ingredients

4 garlic cloves, minced and divided

1/2 teaspoon salt, divided

1/4 teaspoon freshly ground black pepper, divided

5 sun-dried tomatoes, packed without oil, diced

1 (10-ounce) package frozen chopped spinach, thawed, drained, and squeezed dry

1/4 cup (1 ounce) crumbled fat-free feta cheese

3 tablespoons cream cheese

1/2 teaspoon grated lemon rind

4 (4-ounce) boneless center-cut loin pork chops, trimmed

2 tablespoons fresh lemon juice

2 teaspoons Dijon mustard

1/4 teaspoon dried oregano

Directions

Preheat broiler. Heat a large nonstick skillet over medium-high heat. Coat pan with cooking spray.

Add 2 garlic cloves; saute 1 minute. Add 1/4 teaspoon salt, 1/8 teaspoon pepper, tomatoes, and spinach; saute until moisture evaporates.

Remove from heat; stir in cheeses and rind. Cut a horizontal slit through thickest portion of each pork chop to form a pocket. Stuff about 1/4 cup spinach mixture into each pocket.

Sprinkle remaining 1/4 teaspoon salt and remaining 1/8 teaspoon pepper over pork.

Arrange pork on the rack of a broiler pan or roasting pan coated with cooking spray; place rack in pan.

Combine remaining 2 garlic cloves, juice, mustard, and oregano in a bowl; stir well. Brush half of mustard mixture over pork. Broil 6 minutes; turn pork.

Brush remaining mixture over pork; broil 2 minutes or until done.

Nutrition:

Calories 259; Fat 10g; Protein 35g; Carbs 4g; per 1/4 of recipe

Grilled Lemon Pork Chops

Ingredients

1/4 cup lemon juice

2 tablespoons vegetable oil

4 cloves garlic, minced

1 teaspoon salt

1/4 teaspoon dried oregano

1/4 teaspoon pepper

6 (4 ounce) boneless pork loin chops

Directions

In a large resealable bag, combine lemon juice, oil, garlic, salt, oregano, and pepper. Place chops in bag, seal, and refrigerate 2 hours or overnight. Turn bag frequently to distribute marinade.

Preheat an outdoor grill for high heat. Remove chops from bag, and transfer remaining marinade to a saucepan. Bring marinade to a boil, remove from heat, and set aside.

Lightly oil the grill grate. Grill pork chops for 5 to 7 minutes per side, basting frequently with boiled marinade, until done.

Nutrition:

Calories 202; Fat 10g; Protein 25g; Carbs 1g; per 1/6 of recipe

Rosemary Pork Loin Roast

Ingredients

3 cloves garlic, minced

1 tablespoon dried rosemary

salt and pepper to taste

2 pounds boneless pork loin roast

1/4 cup olive oil

1/2 cup white wine

Directions

Preheat oven to 350 degrees F (175 degrees C).

Crush garlic with rosemary, salt and pepper, making a paste. Pierce meat with a sharp knife in several places and press the garlic paste into the openings. Rub the meat with the remaining garlic mixture and olive oil.

Place pork loin into oven, turning and basting with pan liquids. Cook until the pork is no longer pink in the center, about 1 hour. An instant-read thermometer inserted into the center should read 145 degrees F (63 degrees C).

Remove roast to a platter. Heat the wine in the pan and stir to loosen browned bits of food on the bottom. Serve with pan juices.

Nutrition:

Calories 238; Fat 16g; Protein 18g; Carbs 1g; per 1/8 of recipe

Goat Cheese Chicken Breasts

Ingredients

4 oz goat cheese, soft

1 tbsp pepper

5 sprigs dill weed

2 tsp thyme

1 tbsp rosemary

16 oz chicken breast, no skin

Directions

Pound out Chicken Breast Flat and thin and trim edges. Cut into 4 oz servings. Pepper both sides of Chicken.

Cut goat cheese into equal 1 oz portions spread into middle of Chicken along with remaining herbs portioned.

Fold chicken in half. Grill until chicken is done.

Nutrition:

Calories 205; Fat 7g; Protein 31g; Carbs 1.5g; per 1/4 of recipe

25394243R00032

Printed in Great Britain
by Amazon